Explore!
WORLD WAR II

Jane Bingham

WAYLAND

First published in 2014 by Wayland

Copyright © Wayland 2014

Wayland
338 Euston Road
London NW1 3BH

Wayland Australia
Level 17/207 Kent Street
Sydney, NSW 2000

 Produced for Wayland by
White-Thomson Publishing
www.wtpub.co.uk
+44 (0)843 208 7460

Editor: Jane Bingham
Designer: Tim Mayer
Picture researcher: Jane Bingham
Illustrations for step-by-step: Stefan Chabluk
Map: Ian Thompson
Proof reader: Lucy Ross

ISBN 978 0 7502 8038 9

Dewey Number 940.5'3-dc23

Printed in China

Wayland is a division of Hachette Children's Books,
an Hachette UK company

Picture acknowledgements:
The author and publisher would like to thank the
following agencies and people for allowing these
pictures to be reproduced:

Cover (top left) Wikimedia; (top right) Len Green/
Shutterstock; (central panel) caesart/Shutterstock;
(bottom left) Mesut Dogan/Shutterstock; (bottom
right) Wikimedia; p.1 (left) The Illustrated London
News Picture Library/Bridgeman Art Library; (right)
Honourableandbold/Dreamstime; p.3 Naci Yavuz/
Shutterstock; p.4 Gepapix/Dreamstime; p.5 (top)
Philcold/Dreamstime; (bottom) Wikimedia; p.6
Historical/Corbis; p.7 (top) Honourableandbold/
Dreamstime; (bottom) Wikimedia; p.8 Wikimedia;
p.9 (top) Mesut Dogan/Shutterstock; (bottom)
Wikimedia; p.10 Neftali/Shutterstock; p.11 Gnohz/
Dreamstime; p.12 Naci Yavuz/Shutterstock;
p.13 (top) Dutch photographer (20th century)/
Private Collection/Bridgeman Art Library; (bottom)
upthebanner/Shutterstock; p.14 Wikimedia; p.15
(top) Wikimedia; (bottom) Wikimedia; p.16 The
Illustrated London News Picture Library/Bridgeman
Art Library; p.17 (top) Ruthblack/Dreamstime;
(bottom) Wikimedia; p.18 Wikimedia; p.19
Wikimedia; p.20 Darksidephotos/Dreamstime;
p.21 (top) Solarseven/Dreamstime; (middle)
Wikimedia; (bottom) Wikimedia; p.24 Icholakov/
Dreamstime; p.25 (top) Len Green/Shutterstock;
p.25 (bottom) Wikimedia; p.26 dudchik/i-stock;
p.27 (top) dudchik/i-stock; (bottom) Smokon/
Dreamstime; p.28 Sari ONeal/Shutterstock;
p.29 (top) Pixattitude/Dreamstime; (bottom) Jim
Vallee/Shutterstock; p.31 dudchik/i-stock; p.32
Wikimedia.

Contents

What was World War Two?

World War Two lasted from September 1939 to August 1945. Over 30 countries took part in the conflict and by the end of the war, in 1945, around 60 million people had died. Roughly half these deaths were civilians – men, women and children who had not taken part in the fighting.

Adolf Hitler led the Nazi party. He promised the German people that he would make their country rich and powerful.

Why did it begin?

World War Two began when the German leader, Adolf Hitler, ordered his army to invade other countries in Europe. A few nations supported him, but many other countries were determined to stop the German invasions.

During World War Two, fighter pilots fought fierce battles in the skies.

Who fought the war?

Germany's main supporters were Italy and Japan. The Germans and their supporters were known as the Axis powers. Germany's opponents were called the Allies. By the end of the war, there were over 20 Allied nations, including Britain, the Soviet Union and the USA. The Allies fought to prevent Hitler from gaining more power. They also opposed Japan in the Far East.

Death and destruction

The war was fought on land, in the air, on the oceans and under the sea. Major bombing raids were carried out on cities and nuclear bombs were used for the first time. Hitler's Nazi Party was also responsible for the Holocaust. This terrible act of destruction involved the mass murder of over five million Jews.

The war begins

In March 1938 Hitler's troops invaded Austria. Soon the German forces had gained control of Czechoslovakia, and on 1 September 1939 they invaded Poland. Britain and France had promised to defend Poland. They declared war on Germany on 3 September.

Invading France

There was little action for the first six months of the war. Then, in 1940, Hitler launched a powerful attack. German tanks swept rapidly into France and by June they had gained control of much of the country. Meanwhile, thousands of Allied troops were left trapped in northern France. The British organized a massive rescue from the beaches at Dunkirk. In just nine days, 330,000 men were carried across the English Channel back to safety in Britain.

Soldiers board a troop carrier during the rescue from Dunkirk.

The Battle of Britain

The next move in Hitler's plan was to invade Britain. In summer 1940 German planes began to launch bombing raids, but British fighter planes fought back fiercely. This struggle for control of the skies lasted for three months and was called the Battle of Britain. Even though the British had fewer planes than the Germans, they still managed to win.

A modern air display of Battle of Britain planes

The Blitz

The fiercest air attack came in September 1940. Known as the 'Blitz', it involved air raids on London and 15 other British cities. Hitler hoped that the Blitz would force the British to surrender. But they fought back by bombing German cities.

Winston Churchill was British Prime Minister from 1940 to 1945. He insisted that Britain would never surrender.

A worldwide war

By 1941, the fighting had begun to spread around the world. Hitler invaded the Soviet Union in June. His troops advanced steadily and by December they had almost reached Moscow. The Germans fought to gain control of Russian cities but the Russians were determined to resist. The Siege of Leningrad dragged on for two years before the German Army was finally defeated.

The Siege of Leningrad left much of the city in ruins.

The USA joins the war

At the start of the war, the USA declared that it did not want to get involved in the fighting. Then, in December 1941, some US Navy ships were bombed while they were anchored in Pearl Harbor, Hawaii. The next day, the USA declared war on Japan. Hitler had signed an agreement with Japan, so he declared war on the USA.

Fighting in Africa

The Allies fought a fierce campaign against the Germans and Italians in North Africa. In 1942 they won the battle of El Alamein. This victory gave them control of some very important shipping routes. It also provided a base for the Allied invasion of Italy.

Soldiers from all over the world took part in the war. These Australian signallers are sending messages in the Libyan Desert in Africa.

Fighting in Asia

Japan already ruled parts of China, which it had invaded in 1937, and in 1942 Japanese forces swept through Southeast Asia. By June, they had seized control of large parts of Thailand, Malaysia and Indonesia, as well as other islands in the Pacific Ocean. At first Japan seemed unbeatable, but the Allies fought back steadily, and they gradually forced the Japanese troops to retreat.

This monument shows American soldiers capturing the Pacific island of Iwo Jima.

The final stages

In December 1941 the Russian Army began to drive back the German Army. Over the next three years, Russian soldiers slowly advanced across Eastern Europe towards Berlin. Meanwhile, in July 1943, Allied troops began moving north through Italy.

D-day landings

On 6 June 1944 the Allies made a surprise attack on the German Army in northern France. Thousands of Allied soldiers landed on the beaches of Normandy in an event that became known as the D-day landings. The Allies fought their way through France, and in September 1944 they entered Germany.

D-DAY

25 P COMMANDOS LANDING ON GOLD BEACH 6 JUNE 1944

This postage stamp commemorates the D-day landings, when Allied troops arrived in northern France.

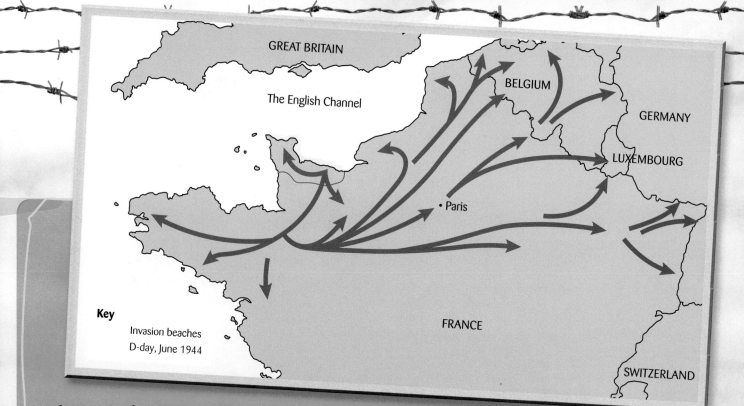

Key

Invasion beaches
D-day, June 1944

Victory in Europe

The Russians reached Berlin, Germany's capital city, in April 1945. Hitler was hiding there, and when he realised that he had been defeated he killed himself. Germany finally surrendered on 8 May 1945. This day became known as VE ('Victory in Europe') day.

This map shows the routes taken by the Allies as they marched through France.

The war ends

Even though the war had ended in Europe, fighting continued in the Pacific region. On 6 August 1945 the USA dropped the world's first atomic bomb on the Japanese city of Hiroshima. It destroyed the city and killed between 60,000 and 80,000 people. Three days later another atomic bomb was dropped on Nagasaki, and Japan surrendered. World War Two had come to an end.

A ruined building in Hiroshima, kept as a memorial to all the victims of the atomic bomb

The Holocaust

After the war ended, Allied soldiers marched into German territory. They were shocked to discover enormous concentration camps where the Nazis had sent Jews, gypsies and the mentally ill. Some prisoners in the camps were forced to work for the Nazis, but millions more were put to death. It has been estimated that as many as 11 million people died in concentration camps in World War Two. This horrific waste of human life is known as the Holocaust.

The Nazis forced all Jews to wear a yellow badge with the word 'Jude' written on it. Jude is German for Jew.

Persecuting the Jews

Hitler's Nazi party began their campaign to persecute the Jews in the 1930s. Jews in Nazi Germany had very few rights and were forced to live apart from other people in areas called ghettos. Gangs of Nazis attacked Jewish people, destroyed their shops and burned down their synagogues.

Hiding from the Nazis

After the war began, Nazi persecution of the Jews became much more extreme. Jewish men, women and children were captured and sent to concentration camps. Many Jewish families tried to hide from the Nazis. A girl called Anne Frank kept a diary about her life in hiding. Today, her diary is read all over the world.

Anne Frank and her family went into hiding when she was 13 years old. She died in a concentration camp when she was 15.

Concentration camps

Jews who had been captured were sent on trains to concentration camps. When they arrived at a camp, men, women and children were separated and only the strongest were allowed to live. All the others were killed in gas chambers.

Auschwitz was the largest of all the concentration camps. Up to three million people died there.

13

On the home front

WAR PRODUCTION CO-ORDINATING COMMITTEE

The war did not only affect the troops. It also changed the lives of those who stayed at home. People of all ages joined in the effort to help their country win the war.

This American poster shows 'Rosie the riveter' working in a factory to help her country.

War work

In Britain, every adult under the age of 51 was registered for war work. Some were employed in munitions factories, making ammunition and weapons. Others worked on farms, growing food to send to the troops. Air-raid wardens kept a watch out for danger, and doctors and nurses cared for the wounded. Women played an important role in the war effort, often taking on the jobs of men who had gone to fight.

Rationing

Once the war began, ships carrying food and other supplies could not reach Britain easily, so there was much less food to go round. Each family had a ration book, with a limited number of coupons to exchange for food. Meat and eggs were in very short supply so people ate mainly tinned meat and powdered eggs. Biscuits and sweets were very strictly rationed. There were no bananas in the shops and the government banned ice cream.

A boy exchanging ration coupons for food

Recycling

In 1940, the British government asked the British people to donate any spare metal for recycling. The metal was made into helmets, grenades and planes. Vast amounts of scrap metal were collected, including iron railings, tin baths, saucepans and keys. Even the Royal Family donated a set of kitchenware to support the war effort.

Women worked on farms to help produce more food. They were known as 'land girls'.

15

Keeping safe

Children being evacuated to the country, carrying their gas masks and a suitcase.

At the start of the war, many people in Britain feared that their country would be invaded. They were especially worried about attacks from the air. The government made plans to send city children to the countryside, where there would be less danger from bombs. These children were called evacuees.

Evacuees

Evacuees were sent to foster homes in country villages. They travelled by train or bus, with a label around their neck saying who they were. When the children arrived at their destination, they were collected by local people and taken home with them. Some children were happy in their foster homes, but many were very homesick.

Bombs and gas

People living in cities were in constant danger from bombing raids. Air-raid wardens sounded a siren to warn everyone that a raid was starting and people took cover in bomb shelters. People also feared gas attacks. Everyone had a gas mask that they had to carry with them at all times.

Some British families built their own bomb shelter in their garden. Anderson shelters like this were covered by a mound of earth. They had room for up to six people.

Blackout

It was very important that towns and cities could not be spotted by enemy bombers, so strict blackout rules were introduced. Windows were covered by heavy curtains or shutters and all the street lights were turned off. Blackout wardens patrolled the streets at night, making sure that they were totally dark.

REEVES

SH-SH-SH-SH-SH

CARELESS TALK

COSTS LIVES

Posters warned people to keep any war news completely secret. There was always the chance that an enemy spy could be listening, and careless talk could put others in danger.

A letter from wartime London

This imaginary letter describes the experiences of a girl living in London during the Blitz. Her letter is written to a friend who has been evacuated to the countryside.

Dear Susie

How is life in the country? I bet it's lovely and peaceful. We have had a hard time here in London. The bombing raids are really heavy, and last week there was a direct hit on our street.

As usual we were woken by the wail of the sirens. We quickly grabbed our gas masks and ran to the nearest Underground station. As we ran through the streets we heard the whistle of falling bombs, followed by a crash as they hit their targets.

The station was crowded with families lying under blankets. Meg, Billy and I all huddled close to Mum. We tried our best to get some sleep but we kept being woken by the sound of explosions.

In the morning we climbed up to the street. There was smoke and dust everywhere, and most of the buildings had been flattened. We wandered through the ruins until we found the place where our house used to be, but all that was left of it was a huge pile of bricks.

Now we are living in a hostel. Mum says it's too dangerous for us to stay in London, so maybe I'll see you soon!

*Love from
Annie*

The letter on this page has been imagined for this book. Can you create your own letter for a child who has been evacuated from wartime London? Use the facts in this book and in other sources to help you write your letter.

19

Science in war

Governments on both sides of the war made use of the latest scientific knowledge. They encouraged scientists to use their skills to help their country win the war.

Radar and sonar

Scientists in Germany, Britain and the USA worked on radar. This new technology made it possible to spot enemy planes and ships from a great distance. Radar transmitters send out radio waves, which bounce off an object and send a signal back again. A similar system, called sonar, was also developed in World War Two. Sonar equipment sends sound waves through water. It was used to locate enemy submarines.

Battleships used radar and sonar equipment to detect enemy ships, planes and submarines.

An atomic bomb

In the early 1940s a team of scientists in the USA developed the atomic bomb. They discovered a way to split the atom (the smallest part of any substance) in order to create a massive explosion. Atomic bombs are also known as nuclear bombs. They create massive amounts of heat and energy and cause much greater damage than any other bomb.

People were horrified by the destruction caused by atomic bombs in World War Two. Since then, no nuclear bombs have been used in war.

Code makers and breakers

Both sides in the war used secret codes to send their messages. Teams of computer scientists and mathematicians built special machines to scramble all the letters used in a message. The Germans made a famous Enigma code machine that could create an endless number of codes. They believed their machine was unbeatable, but Allied code breakers worked day and night until they understood how it worked.

The Enigma machine looked like an ordinary typewriter, but it contained a mechanism to change all the letters in a message.

Send a coded message

Why not try sending coded messages to your friends? Instead of using a complex Enigma machine, you can use a simple cipher wheel. (Cipher is another word for code.) Follow the instructions to make and use a cipher wheel.

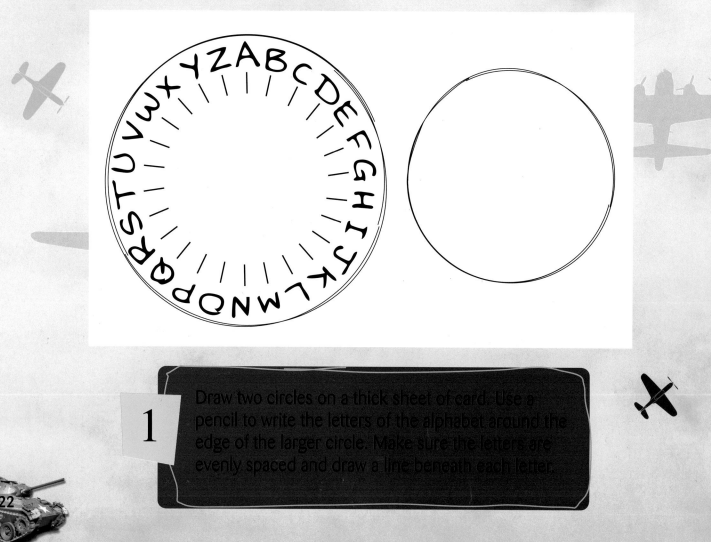

1 Draw two circles on a thick sheet of card. Use a pencil to write the letters of the alphabet around the edge of the larger circle. Make sure the letters are evenly spaced and draw a line beneath each letter.

2 Cut out the two circles and pin them together. Then write the letters of the alphabet around the edge of the inner wheel, making sure they are directly beneath the letters of the outer wheel.

3 Imagine that the letters of the alphabet are numbered 1 to 26. So A=1, B=2, C=3 etc. Then choose a secret number between 1 and 26. Work out which letter this is on the inner wheel, and turn this letter to line up with the A on the outer wheel. If your secret number is 6, move the inner wheel F to line up with outer letter A.

4 To create a coded message, spell out the message on the outer wheel and write down the letters beneath them on the inner wheel. Your friends can only work out the message if you give them the secret number!

Technology in war

During the course of World War Two, designers from rival nations competed with each other to create the most efficient weapons and fighting machines. Many advances in technology were made between the years 1939 and 1945.

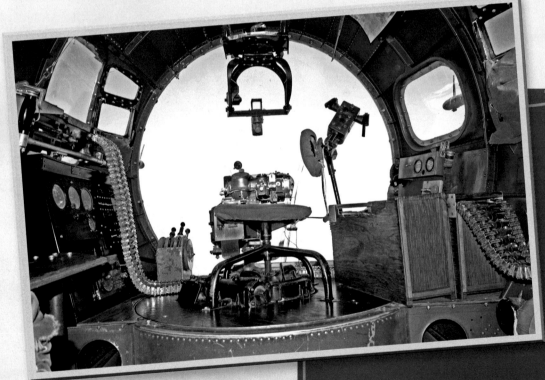

This photo shows a gunner's seat inside a bomber plane. The gun is mounted on a stand and a target-finder helps the gunner to aim at enemy aircraft.

Aircraft

Military aircraft included small fighter planes, such as the German Messerschmitt and the British Spitfire, powerful bombers, and planes used for spying. Aircraft carriers allowed planes to take off from ships in the ocean. Aircraft were made from lightweight aluminium and by the end of the war some jet-powered planes had been developed.

Tanks

Tanks were first used in World War One. The early tanks often broke down, but by the start of World War Two both sides had vehicles that could travel for hundreds of kilometres. During the course of the war, tanks became much heavier in order to resist more powerful weapons. Guns were mounted on a turret that could swivel in all directions.

The American M24 tank was first used in 1944. It was lighter than most of the earlier tanks, and was equipped with a very powerful main gun.

V-weapons

In the 1940s German scientists developed a set of guided weapons that could find their target without a pilot. They were known as V-weapons and included the V-1, a guided bomb, and the V-2, a guided rocket. From 1943 to 1945, V-1 and V-2 weapons were launched at Britain, causing serious damage and loss of life.

A German V-1 bomb on display at a military museum. The British nicknamed the V-1s 'doodlebugs' or 'buzz bombs'.

Picturing the war

There are countless images and records for World War Two. Artists, writers and photographers recorded life in the battle zones and on the home front. Soldiers and civilians wrote letters and diaries, and thousands of documentaries, books and films tell the story of the war.

Paintings like this give a powerful sense of the drama and action of war.

Stories of war

Some war stories have been written especially for children. *The Boy in the Striped Pyjamas* by John Boyne is set in Germany. It tells the story of a friendship between the son of a Nazi officer and a Jewish boy in a concentration camp. *The Amazing Story of Adolphus Tips* by Michael Morpurgo describes the D-day landings in 1944. It is written from the point of view of a British girl and her cat.

Artists' views

Many artists and photographers were paid by their governments to record the conflict. Some showed scenes of fighting, some illustrated the damage caused by bombs, and some concentrated on life on the home front. The British artist and sculptor Henry Moore made a series of drawings of people in the Blitz, taking shelter in London Underground stations.

Remembering the war

After the war was over, memorials were built in many parts of the world to honour the memory of the dead. Some simply have a list of names. Some have figures of soldiers, and some show civilians. These memorials help us to remember the horror of World War Two and the bravery of those who died in the conflict.

This memorial sculpture commemorates the children of Lidice in Czechoslovakia. In 1942, Nazi soldiers destroyed Lidice and killed almost all its people.

Facts and figures

World War Two involved more countries, killed more people, cost more money and damaged more buildings than any other war in history.

US Marines in the Pacific used the Native American Navajo language as their secret code. The Navajo word for 'hummingbird' was the code name for a fighter plane.

Between 50 and 70 million people died in World War Two. Over half of those killed were civilians.

It has been estimated that 11 million people died in the Holocaust. Around six million of the victims were Jews.

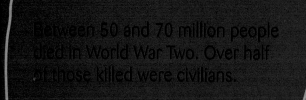

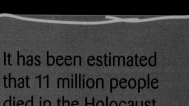

The character of James Bond was partly based on Dusko Popov, a Yugoslavian spy. His code name was 'Tricycle' and he worked for the Allies. Popov spoke at least five languages and invented a recipe for invisible ink.

During World War Two more than 100 million people served in military units. These units came from 30 different countries.

The swastika was adopted by the Nazis as their symbol, but its history dates back thousands of years. The ancient civilizations of Greece, Egypt, China and India all used the swastika as a symbol of good fortune.

Glossary

air raid A bombing attack from planes.

Allies The countries that fought against Germany, Japan and Italy in World War Two.

ammunition Bullets, bombs and other explosives.

atomic bomb A bomb that is created by splitting an atom. Atomic bombs are also known as nuclear bombs.

Blitz The German bombing campaign on London in World War Two.

campaign A series of actions intended to achieve an aim.

commemorate To do something special in memory of a person or an event.

concentration camp A camp where Jews and other victims of the Nazis were imprisoned and often killed.

evacuate To remove people from a place of danger to somewhere safe.

evacuee Someone who is sent from a dangerous to a safe place.

foster home A home where children are looked after by adults other than their parents.

gas chamber A room deliberately filled with poisonous gas as a means of execution.

Holocaust The deliberate killing of Jews and other victims during World War Two.

London Underground The system of trains that run in tunnels underneath the city of London.

memorial A monument created to commemorate someone or something.

Nazi The political party founded and led by Adolf Hitler. Nazi is short for National Socialist Party.

nuclear To do with the splitting of atoms.

persecute To treat someone cruelly and unfairly because of prejudice.

rival Someone who competes against another person.

siege The military action of surrounding a place and waiting for its inhabitants to surrender.

siren A loud warning noise.

surrender To give up in a fight and admit defeat.

synagogue A building used by Jews for worship.

territory An area of land.

transmitter A piece of equipment that sends out signals.

turret A rotating gun platform on top of a tank.

Further reading

In the Second World War (Men, Women and Children), Peter Hepplewhite (Wayland, 2012)

World War II (Craft Box), Jillian Powell (Wayland, 2013)

World War II (True Stories), Clive Gifford (Wayland, 2013)

World War II (What They Don't Tell You About), Robert Fowke (Wayland, 2013)

World War II (Mad, Bad and Just Plain Dangerous), John Townsend (Franklin Watts, 2013)

Websites

http://www.bbc.co.uk/history/worldwars/wwtwo/

A BBC website written by subject experts. It includes video and audio clips, animated maps and sections on code breakers and spies.

http://www.bbc.co.uk/schools/primaryhistory/world_war2/

A BBC website designed for children. The site help you imagine what life was like for children during the war. It has video and audio clips, real letters and a 'time capsule' detective game.

http://homeworkhelp.stjohnssevenoaks.com/Britain.html

An easy-to-follow guide to World War Two. It includes sections on the Blitz, evacuation, posters, and wartime songs.

Index

Who were the Victorians?
Queen Victoria's reign
Empire and exploration
Rich and poor
Working life
Health and medicine
A Victorian schoolchild's diary
Scientists and inventors
Engineers and builders
All kinds of transport
Artists, writers and photographers
Make a thaumatrope
Facts and figures

978 0 7502 8037 2

Who were the Romans?
The rise of Rome
A mighty power
The Roman world
Town and country
Family and school
Religion and worship
A Roman child's day
Entertainment and leisure
Building technology
Artists and writers
Make a mosaic
Facts and figures

978 0 7502 8098 3

What was World War One?
The war begins
A terrible struggle
A worldwide war
A soldier's day
New technology
Send a message in Morse code
Planes, airships and submarines
Women at war
On the home front
Picturing the war
After the war
Facts and figures

978 0 7502 8027 3

Who were the Ancient Egyptians?
Early kingdoms
A mighty power
The Egyptian world
Religion and beliefs
Everyday life
A day at a temple school
Feasting and fun
Brilliant buildings
Medicine, science and magic
Art, music and writing
Write in hieroglyphics
Facts and figures

978 0 7502 8097 6

What was World War Two?
The war begins
A worldwide war
The final stages
The holocaust
On the home front
Keeping safe
A letter from wartime London
Science in war
Send a coded message
Technology in war
Picturing the war
Facts and figures

978 0 7502 8038 9

Who were the Ancient Greeks?
Early Greeks
A great civilization
The Greek world
Family life
Gods and goddesses
Games and plays
A day at the Olympic Games
Make a theatrical mask
Maths, science and medicine
Architects and builders
Art and ideas
Facts and figures

978 0 7502 8099 0

Who were the Tudors?
Two powerful kings
Edward, Mary, Elizabeth
Rich and poor
A kitchen-maid's day
Making Tudor gingerbread
Tudor towns
Tudor entertainments
Exploring the world
Traders and settlers
Science and technology
Artists, musicians and writers
Facts and figures

978 0 7502 8036 5

Who was William Shakespeare?
Young William
A great success
All sorts of plays
Shakespeare's England
The wider world
Shakespeare's London
The Globe Theatre
Make a model theatre
Actors and playwrights
A boy actor's day
Music and art
Facts and figures

978 0 7502 8135 5